Mora

A. C. GRAYLING

PHŒNIX

A PHOENIX PAPERBACK

First published in Great Britain in 1997 by
Phoenix, a division of the Orion Publishing Group Ltd
Orion House
5 Upper Saint Martin's Lane
London, WC2H 9EA

A CIP catalogue record for this book is available
from the British Library.

ISBN 0 297 81973 9

Typeset by SetSystems Ltd, Saffron Walden
Set in 9/13.5 Stone Serif
Printed in Great Britain by
Clays Ltd St Ives plc

PREDICTIONS

Contents

Preface
Predicting the Moral Future

Prediction is a mug's game. Consider horse-racing: you can be an experienced punter who exactly knows the form and going, but your horse might lose nevertheless. Yet this is a simple species of prediction where chances are calculable. It is infinitely otherwise with social attitudes and practices, where 'chaotic' effects – in the mathematical sense of small initial factors ramifying into large differences later – apply to already complex questions. The difficulty increases when one adds the fact that, in thinking about moral values, there is a close relationship between saying how things might be and how things should be – at very least because when one says 'matters will probably be thus' one is immediately tempted to add either 'and so they should' or 'they should be otherwise'; for moral debate is not a neutral matter, but concerns the realm of action, choice, and the character of life, where bare description never seems enough.

Given the difficulties, how can one venture to make predictions about morality? One might suppose that as history is, at least to some extent, the mirror of the future, one might seek there for instruction. There is some truth in this; but, on such large questions as the moral evolution of societies, the derivable lessons tend to be general, often ambiguous, and sometimes contradictory. Moral history can seem endlessly cyclical, with periods of austerity succeeding relative liberalism, which in turn liberalize after a time, only to retrench again. Sometimes there seems to be an inertia in human affairs, reversing progress at every opportunity of war or disaster. But such remarks are tendentious; history, including moral history, never exactly repeats itself; and nothing is ever quite lost from the argument of time. Moreover there is always a danger of our reading present value-judgements back into the record; for example, commentators used to say that, in its successful republican youth, Rome was austere and chaste, and that the voluptuousness of its later imperial stages was a symptom of decline. When we do this, history cannot teach us about our future, for it is (absurdly) being made to take lessons from our present.

But there is indeed something to be learned from the history of morality. It is that it consists in a struggle – a Heraclitean one, as the flux back and forth shows, and a Herculean one, given how much of the happiness of mankind is at stake – between what, for brevity, one might call 'liberal' and 'conservative' values. I speak of the history of the Western world – the world of essentially European and Judaeo-Christian origin. The only safe prediction about the future of morality in this world is that it will continue the self-same struggle, with no real ascendancy between either party, but with each thinking that the other is ascendant – and occasionally, to the real distress of the other, with one of them temporarily being so. Most people, as individuals, never belong fully to either party, but hover between, tending to err on the liberal side in respect of their own conduct and on the conservative side in respect of others' conduct. One large difference between the parties is that when the conservatives have the upper hand they actively persecute the liberals (in the past going so far as to burn them at the stake), whereas the liberals, when ascendant, cause conservatives no greater agonies than those of disapproval and chagrin.

But there is something else to be said about the future, the most important thing of all. This is that it does not exist: it waits to be made. Therefore the future of morality depends upon what we choose it to be. It is not there, laid like railway tracks running forward into time, for us helplessly to trundle along them, surprised or dismayed by what comes into view. As masters of the future, our duty is to think as clearly as we can about what kind of people we wish to be and what kind of life we wish to lead; and then to choose, and to act, as wisely as we may.

As a contribution to choosing the future, the rest of this essay sets out the conservative and liberal views – firmly on the side of the latter, for to repeat: morality is not a neutral matter – not in predictive, but in polemic mode. I return to the question of prediction at the very end.

Chapter 1
Introduction

This is an essay in moralizing, not in moral philosophy. It is a brief essay, and therefore summary. The questions it addresses are complicated and delicate, and have been, and continue to be, discussed in the wider debate that society has with itself in many different forums, from academic seminars to newspaper columns and beyond. This is a contribution to that debate, and presupposes it; but it is also an argument for a change of perspective, which if accepted would help to change the debate's terms.

The difference between moral philosophy and moralizing merits comment. Some moral philosophers deny that it is their job to moralize – that is, to offer guidance, and to say how one should choose and act – on the ground that they are no better fitted to do so than anyone else. Instead they see their task as clarification of the concepts used in moral debate (for chief examples: 'goodness', 'right', 'duty' and 'obligation'), together with investigation of the reasoning employed about them. Moral philosophy thus conceived is a neutral, purely descriptive task, which studiously avoids offering views about how to live.

This is a recent development. Past moral philosophers were concerned to identify and enjoin the good life, and to recommend ways of resolving the problems whose occurrence is guaranteed by the complexity of human existence. Given the three facts that life is a demanding business, that many search for guidance in how to live it, and that most who offer to guide them do so from tendentious religious or political standpoints, it seems not just a pity, but a dereliction, that moral philosophy has turned its back; for philosophy is the enterprise of reason, which tries to take the large, clear view, guided by logic and the facts – from which, therefore, one might reasonably hope for more judicious results than partisan faiths or factions can offer.

In any case, moralizing needs moral philosophy. In moralizing one has to reason from principles, which in turn require grounds. Although what follows is an act of moralizing, it therefore also includes at least something of its justification.

Most of what I say will be regarded as mere common sense by some, and as highly controversial by others. Past example shows that it is hard to persuade the latter to think and behave differently; but the argument with them must be continued nevertheless, for their views remain influential – and, arguably, harmful.

To most, discussion of morality suggests discussion of a familiar range of topics: the family, sex, drugs, crime; the implications of medical advances; standards in public life. But this perception of what matters most is not universal. It is chiefly believed in the Anglo-Saxon West, in Muslim countries and in China. This geo-social remark is intended to give pause, as reminding us that in (for example) non-Anglo-Saxon Europe, especially northern Europe, not all of the problems listed, least of all sex and drugs, seem quite so acute; not because people there indulge less in either, but because they are more tolerant of both. A comparative study of moral attitudes among the world's societies would indeed be instructive, among other things showing that one reason why North America and Britain differ from continental Europe in the noted respect is that more austere, less tolerant varieties of Protestant Christianity have been influential there. It might also show that where Christian or Muslim missionaries have not penetrated, the peoples of Africa, South America and the Pacific islands perceive the moral realm differently – as they still do in India, and once did in pre-Communist China.

These generalizations are intended to keep before us the thought that moralities are socially constructed and historically shaped. It is healthy to remember that what is taboo or acceptable in one culture might be the reverse in another. At very least, that fact should make one keenly re-examine one's own values.

The Great Moral Questions

But the great moral questions – the most important and urgent ones – are not about sex, drugs and unmarried mothers. They are, instead, about human rights, war, the arms trade, poverty in the Third World, and inequality and injustice everywhere. These areas of concern involve truly staggering horrors and human sufferings. In comparison to them, the parochial and largely misguided anxieties over sex, drugs and the other matters that fill newspapers and agitate the 'Moral Majority' in America and Britain, pale into triviality. It is itself a moral scandal that these questions preoccupy debate in comfortable corners of the world, while real atrocity and oppression exist elsewhere. This is not to deny that the parochial concerns are important, for they are: but, as I shall argue below, their importance lies in what is almost invariably the opposite of what moral conservatives think.

The claim that human rights violations, war and Third World poverty are the greatest of moral problems hardly needs explanation or justification. The piteous agonies of refugees, the starving, the massacred, the tortured, the imprisoned, are eloquent in their own case. It is astonishing how many in the world's comfortable regions are nightly able to witness the plight of their fellow humans, only to turn off their television sets and forget what they saw. Perhaps the reason is that individuals feel helpless in the face of so much and such profound suffering. Beyond making a donation to a suitable charity – and there is a reasonable limit to what one can give – the next step in active concern threatens to consume too much of one's time and resources, thereby disrupting one's own projects in life.

This suggests that it is better for governments to take action, as the collective agency of the people they serve. Impelled by their electorates, they could, and on this view should, act in concert to halt those among their number who violate their citizens' rights, or make war. The United Nations organization embodies a noble aspiration to this end; but in practice it is enfeebled by its members' divisions and its lack of funds, so that the good it does is limited. But it still does good at times, not least in representing ideals – among which its Universal Declaration of Human Rights is central.

Human Rights
When the UN came into existence at the end of the Second World War one of its earliest acts was to respond to the appalling atrocities of the preceding years by boldly committing itself to the ideal of treating every human individual in the world as possessed of basic rights, and of trying to protect those rights. The Charter of the UN, adopted in 1945, affirmed 'faith in fundamental human rights, in the dignity and worth of the person, and in the equal rights of

men and women and of nations large and small'. Accordingly the UN established a committee to draft a Universal Declaration. The committee worked swiftly, and the Declaration was adopted in 1948 without a dissenting vote. At the time it was particularly welcomed by Third World countries and subjects of colonial rule. Since then the Universal Declaration has been supplemented by two Covenants, respectively on political and civil rights and on social and economic rights, and dozens of further international instruments, jointly constituting an International Bill of Human Rights.

It might seem that these resolutions have little practical worth, because human rights violations continue everywhere in the world, often in the grossest forms. Yet their mere existence has unquestionably reduced the number and severity of violations, and gives powerful aid to individuals and groups opposing them, as witness the patient endeavours of non-governmental organizations at the annual sessions in Geneva of the United Nations' Commission on Human Rights. Progress is slow – painfully so, usually – but it represents a striking historical departure. One of its chief effects is that the International Bill of Human Rights now weighs significantly in international legal proceedings. This is one of the most optimistic signs for the world's future.

The Universal Declaration is a bold document. It starts from the claim that 'all members of the human family' enjoy 'inherent dignity and equal and inalienable rights' and that upon the recognition of this rests our best hopes of achieving the great universal desiderata of freedom, justice and peace. Disregard for these rights led to the barbarities of the Second World War, vivid in the memory of the international community, which, as it emerged from their shadow, sought to renew its hopes for 'a world in which human beings shall enjoy freedom of speech and belief and freedom from fear and want'. Recognizing that such aspirations merit the protection of law, the UN's Declaration sets out to describe what that law should encompass. The chief provisions are that all human beings are born free and equal in rights; that these latter include life, liberty, and security, freedom from slavery and cruel punishment, recognition before and protection by law, freedom of movement, freedom to express views, to participate in the government of the state, to have an education, to own property, to practise a religion, to have time for leisure, to make choices in personal life, and to enjoy peace. Correlatively, the Declaration recognizes that everyone has duties to others and to the community, which in sum make it possible for others to enjoy the same rights also.

These principles by now seem commonplace to people in the West, for whom they state a mere minimum of expectation. But to the majority of the world's population they are still ideals rather than realities, and for anyone languishing in political detention, or in the shadow of a harsh regime, they represent precious aspirations. Philosophical discussion of the basis and justification of rights continues; but one could abbreviate it by *laying claim* to those rights, defending one's arrogation of them on the ground that history has taught us what best promotes human flourishing, and that enjoyment of these rights is essential to it.

One main purpose of ethics might be to help people see that human rights are chief among the moral issues facing the world, and to urge them to act accordingly. People need only decide to do something about the problems thus identified; at the very least to write, and to keep on writing, to their political representatives, demanding collective action; and voting accordingly – and never forgetting that the truly important moral questions lie here. If there is an arena where the greatest challenges for the future lie, and with them therefore the greatest need for moral heroism and endeavour, it is in the sphere of human rights. The development of science and technology shows us that, as a species, we have grown clever; their misuse for war and oppression shows us that we have not yet grown wise. Moral heroism is required for us to teach ourselves wisdom.

I shall say no more about the great question of human rights here, because it speaks for itself. There are other social and political questions of relevance to ethics that do not always speak for themselves; in particular, those about poverty and inequality cannot be left aside, because in all their forms they touch the nerve of debates about the good life in the good society. Accordingly I mention them again below.

'Morality' and 'Ethics'

The remainder of what follows treats of some of the standard and familiar problems in moral debate, involving what are seen as threats to 'family values' and allied concerns, which for most people, as noted, turn on questions about marriage and divorce, sexual practices and behaviour, drug abuse, and such dilemmas as abortion and euthanasia. This list is not exhaustive, but it covers central ground.

It helps to recognize a distinction between narrow definitions of 'morality' as conceived in modern times (chiefly since the eighteenth century) and a more inclusive, classical conception of 'ethics'. As the notion now operates, morality applies just to parts of life, chiefly to interpersonal relationships; and it invariably concerns such matters as marital infidelity and malicious gossip. No one thinks that eating bananas is a moral matter, nor how a person works, or what colour he paints his house. The philosophers of classical antiquity thought differently. For them all of life is an ethical matter: one lives and does well as a whole person, and both one's flourishing and effect on others flow from one's total character. For this reason life has to be considered – 'the unconsidered life', said Socrates, 'is not worth living' – and it can only be considered if it is informed.

Questions about ethics, therefore, as against those having to do with more narrowly conceived morality, are questions about intelligent human flourishing – which is to say: human well-being and well-doing. They therefore seek answers not only to questions about what sort of people we should be, but about what sort of society we should have – so that the best we can aspire to be can have the best environment to thrive in. Thus ethics and politics, as Aristotle saw, are continuous.

Grasping the distinction between morality and ethics is important because it helps us to promote the latter. Morality is about what is allowed and forbidden in particular realms of behaviour; ethics is about the character of one's personality and life. Therefore the groundwork of ethics is not rules and codes, admonitions and sanctions, as in morality, but an education of character whose primary target is the inculcation of thoughtfulness, insight, taste and tolerance. The admittedly utopian conviction thus embodied is that from success in such an enterprise ethical society will grow; and in such a society the permissions and prohibitions with which morality concerns itself will be unnecessary because already comprised in the mutual respect and tolerance constituting the relationships among its members.

I turn to these larger considerations later. The best way of showing why they are worth promoting is to work through the main moral (in the narrow sense) debates that bedevil Western societies. Discussing them shows that the moral problems we think we face change character when viewed from what in the end is seen as an ethical perspective.

Two Facts and Two Demands

Most people are capable at times of being well judging and careful, and able to think things through in a generous frame of mind. In such moods one can recognize two facts, and two demands entailed by them, which are profoundly important to ethical considerations – and yet which are, as is often the case with profundities, simple.

The first fact is that we (for *any* 'we') have a good idea of what, in a general way, conduces to human flourishing. One can interpret the Universal Declaration of Human Rights as stating that understanding in full, but it can be put more summarily. Shelter, warmth, food, companion-ship, health, freedom, security: this is easily the list of desiderata which – irrespective of their historical or cultural setting – most people would acknowledge as among the necessities of a good life. Of course there is much more, of more complex and diverse kinds, that make for full human flourishing, for humans are intelligent and creative animals: all the arts and sciences, and the various amenities of civilization, show what we have found attractive besides.

The second fact might at first seem to conflict with the

first. It is that there is a great variety of human interests, not all of which one can be confident of understanding. No one can see things from everyone else's point of view; few can expect to achieve real insight into the needs and desires of others merely on the basis of knowing their own.

The conflict between the two facts is merely apparent. A relativist might dispute the first by saying that, if we think we know what people elsewhere or at other times regard as desirable, we risk misinterpreting them according to our own parochial views. But this argument is at best only half right, for the first fact is that we have a perfectly good general understanding of what makes for human flourishing, even if – as the second fact then adds – we have to learn more to discover what is sufficient for such flourishing on an individual basis, taking background considerations into account.

Two demands follow immediately from these two facts. The first is that if we know the least of what makes for the flourishing of others, then, if those others lack it – or are offered the opposite of it by, say, oppressors or natural disaster – this makes a call on us. To know that another is without the minimum that makes for human flourishing, and to ignore the fact, is wrong – or at very least, deeply imprudent; for, in a world in which people recognize others' needs but ignore them, one will oneself be sure to suffer as a result. Therefore, even on minimal prudential grounds, people do well to act in such a way that this is not a world in which we perceive but ignore each other's needs. (Below I give grounds for saying that it is not merely imprudent but unethical, in the inclusive classical sense, to act this way.)

The second demand is that, when we recognize the variety of human needs and desires, our first step must be to tolerate that variety, because it is so great that, as noted, we cannot always expect to have a ready insight into it; so the only way to avoid being mistaken, or prejudiced, or motivated by ignorance, is to be open-minded. Again the point can be substantiated by appeal even to the lowest motivation. We each wish to live our own lives and make our own choices, and in doing so to be respected or at least tolerated by others. We wish for sufficient latitude from others to carry out our own projects, even when they do not understand what our projects mean to us. Because we wish this to be a world where this happens, we have to extend the same consideration to others.

The Limits of Tolerance

This generosity is premised, as noted, on the insight that we cannot expect to understand, without sympathy and the right kind of effort at least, people whose concerns are different from our own, especially if they inhabit other conditions or cultures. But this is not mere mindless tolerance; it is neither unqualified nor irrevocable. For there are intolerable acts – murder, rape, torture, oppression, warmongering and injustice – whose perpetrators, whoever they are, step absolutely beyond the pale. This suggests a familiar principle: that whatever anyone does, he should be free to do it provided it does not harm others, and allows them to pursue their own goals under the same condition. This principle only says what one must not do – namely, that one must not interfere with or harm others. The first demand is stronger, having the form of a positive injunction: it says that we should help others when we recognize their need.

All this implies that the great sin is harm to people (which includes failing to help when one sees the need).

One should say: the great sin is harm to other sentient creatures; but, although this is correct, I shall restrict discussion to humans here, for it is at least clear that they have a special place among sentient creatures, as having closer interests to our own, and as being capable of more various kinds of suffering.

I characterized the two demands at their lowest denominators, to show that even if we are merely self-regarding it is prudential to obey those demands. But of course I believe that we do far better with an ethics which adds other-regardingness to self-regardingness. This is done by recognizing and respecting others' interests, so that by a thoughtful mutual navigation of concerns we always seek the best, and at times accept the least bad, for ourselves and each other, taken together. The justification is that living thus is more satisfying and fruitful for everyone concerned than if one met these demands merely out of self-interest; and the kind of world in which most people felt this way would be a better-quality world than one in which mere self-interest prompts us to tolerate, and occasionally to help, others when it is useful to ourselves to do so. For one would not always find it useful to help others; indeed, the imperatives of competition and advantage-seeking would often make it harmful to oneself to tolerate or help others; so such a world would only be patchily mutual at best – and, even then, for not very edifying reasons. It has to be admitted, alas, that this describes our world as it is.

These remarks touch on matters of importance in several further ways. They bear on a truth that gives much of the point to ethical and political debate, recognized as seamlessly connected. This is that in human communities both resources and sympathies are limited; that competition between individuals and groups is therefore inevitable, and can, and often does, lead to conflict; and that therefore we need laws, rules and traditions to ameliorate our relationships, and to resolve conflicts. On the front line of these are ethical considerations, which enjoin a certain mutual attitude between people – of respect, consideration and trust-keeping; of kindness where appropriate and fellowship where possible – and which constitute the reasons for a person's acting in one way rather than another when his actions affect others.

With these thoughts to hand, we can now turn to the standard questions of moral debate.

Chapter 2
'Family Values' and Values

Most debate about morality clusters around a set of problems, or perceived problems, which are most easily identified by the proposed ideal with respect to which they are thought to fall short, namely, the morality of 'family values'. The concept of a model family and its behaviour is central to this view. That model is of a happy nuclear family of two parents, one of either sex, with obedient, well-socialized offspring, living together in the same household into which others come only by arrangement and temporarily. None of the family use illegal drugs, and if they use legal ones (alcohol, nicotine) they do so moderately and sensibly. The parents limit their sexual interest to one another, and the offspring engage in sexual activity only when, as adults in their turn, they have committed themselves to a responsible relationship – standardly, a permanent monogamous marriage – with a member of the opposite sex. This family is economically independent, socially responsible, law-abiding and observant of contemporary norms.

That is the minimum that a model 'family values' family should be. More evangelical supporters of this ethos urge us, in addition, to be against abortion, homosexuality, divorce, pornography, and too much welfarism (on the grounds that people should take responsibility for themselves), and in favour of hanging and other very severe punishments for crime. They also strongly oppose the use of drugs – some of them include the legal drugs too, as temperance and prohibition movements show. Many supporters of 'family values' justify all these views on religious grounds.

This ethos is complex and interesting. Arguably, it is a mixture of something right and much wrong, the latter stemming from traditions of thought – principally religious – which are themselves complex.

What is right about this conservative ethos is that it recognizes, and makes central, the value of settled domestic affections, by which I mean those that sustain long-term, committed, co-operative relationships based on affection and shared interests at the core of private life. Without doubt such affections, as found in the happiest marriages and most flourishing families, are a great good. It is scarcely needful to list their benefits. But such affections can be, and are, enjoyed in a large variety of ways, of which the 'family values' model family is only one, and – as its short history shows – a rather unsuccessful one. Moreover, the 'family values' school takes its attitudes to sex and sexuality, marriage and fertility, drugs, crime and the nature of society, to be the corollary of their belief in the nuclear-family version of what promotes domestic affections. This, arguably, is a mistake – and sometimes a tragic one, as we can see from the number of social problems it causes. Conservative morality, in other words, is the problem, not the solution, in much that causes difficulty in society. This is because it is repressive and prohibitive in ways that cut across the grain of human nature. As a first step to seeing why, consider the family in 'family values'.

The Nuclear Family

The nuclear family is the 'family values' preferred model. Of relatively recent origin – it is a Western urban industrial phenomenon – it is proving notoriously unsuccessful, because it suffers both structural and ethical flaws. The structural flaw is best described by contrast with what it replaces. For much of history the typical family was (and elsewhere in the world still is) a small community, often consisting of more than two generations of people not always related to each other genetically or by marriage, in which the caretaking of children was effected chiefly by other children, grandparents, servants or economically unproductive (because, say, disabled) members of the household. In such families incest was by no means uncommon (if a man's wife were pregnant or menstruating he might turn to his eldest daughter), and the associated facts of life – disease, mortality, poverty – were familiars. Death gave family life a character quite different from how it now is in the West; it made most childhoods and marriages short.

In the 'family values' nuclear family, psychological and physical burdens are borne by a small inwardly focused group. Traditional extended families were diffuse in structure, offering varieties of channels for managing emotions and resolving conflicts; but the nuclear family intensifies both by diverting them all inwards. To this structural flaw is added an ethical flaw relating to the principles that govern the relationships in this enclosed small group. This is that these relationships are intended to be both permanent and exclusive. Divorce and adultery (not to say the even more problematic ways of relieving the claustrophobia – and hence tensions – of nuclear family life, such as drunkenness, violence and incest) are strongly disapproved of, so not only is the group cooped up together in a small emotional space, but the exits and safety-valves for the resulting pressures are blocked. The results are familiar enough: 'family breakdown' is a lamented commonplace, on which many social ills are blamed. It is a tribute to the human capacity for deceit and self-denial that complete breakdown occurs in 'only' one out of two or three nuclear families, although one does not know what greater costs are sometimes paid in keeping nuclear families together.

In an effort to shore up this inherently unstable family model, the conservative ethic has to stigmatize much that is neutral or even good across the whole range of interpersonal relations and private recreations, not least among them sexuality. The chief aim is to contain the pressures that threaten to explode the nuclear family, if possible by persuading people not to feel them in the first place, but anyway forbidding their expression. A nuclear family works where one of the marital partners is submissive or compromising, and the children are dutiful – and, say, a religious commitment has imposed strong internal controls on temptations that might disrupt these attitudes and the bonds they sustain. A family nourished on religious doctrines which encourage such an outlook is exactly the 'family values' ideal. But it is immediately obvious that it is premised on self-denials and beliefs for which there are no independently good reasons; the only reason for their acceptance is to protect the 'family values' family from breaking down. Urging them, therefore, is rather like urging someone to give up breathing on the grounds that he will never thereafter catch 'flu.

Divorce and Marriage

Because the modern nuclear family figures so importantly in their outlook, moral conservatives are hostile to divorce, which represents the termination – in their view the failure – of a nuclear-family project. Yet divorce is often a good thing; it gives people a chance to start again, or – which is as great a good, if people could only recognize it as such – to live alone: solitary life is not necessarily lonely life, but can be a strong and productive mode of existence, and very peaceful.

Divorce allows freedom and flexibility for everyone, but especially for women, to make changes when change is needed in their domestic arrangements. Marriage without the possibility of divorce is a life-sentence based on decisions made (usually) at a time when the participants' judgement was immature, and anyway influenced by pheromones or fashions. Without divorce, the result is unchangeable, no matter what new circumstances arise. Divorce is often a miserable experience because it signals the loss of affections important to one or both parties; but it is even more wretched when society makes divorce difficult, so adding to the problems of those experiencing it.

Like abortion, divorce is a question of personal freedom. It is about people starting afresh, remedying mistakes, getting back on course with other decisions and choices, to construct lives worth living.

There would be no divorce if there were no marriage. Marriage is a central pillar of the 'family values' view, not merely in the desirable sense of a long-term committed relationship, but as a legally constituted one which controls the age and sex of the parties to it (it says who can enter it, and when), and dictates what they can and must do in it, and on what terms, if any, they can leave it. So viewed, legal marriage looks like a monstrous public interference in personal relations, and it is surprising how many people still go in for it. Aside from their religious interests (and – more trivially – the fun of dressing up for the ceremony, the usefulness of getting presents, or the unmeaning claim that 'getting married shows commitment'), couples asked why, instead of just living together, they choose legal marriage tend, to cite the interests of children they might have. Bastardy considerations might once have made sense of this point, but are an irrelevance now.

The truth, no doubt, is that people continue to marry merely because it is traditional and in so doing they perpetuate an institution which originated for inequitable social and economic reasons, chief among them to control the sexual activity and fertility of women, and thus to ensure that the property men bequeath has a better chance of going to children who are truly theirs.

One-Parent Families

But questions about children's interests always touch a chord, and are therefore important to 'family values' supporters, not only in their defence of nuclear-family marriage but in their correlative attack on one-parent families. Children's interests, they claim, are served best by the former and are at risk in the latter.

Is this true? What matters to children is love, stability, a good diet and opportunities to play and learn. It does not matter how many parents they have or even whether the person or people who look after them are their biological parents, so long as the relationship is a secure and permanent one. Biological parturition is no guarantee of the social skills required for parenting.

The problem with one-parent families is the absence not of one parent, but of resources – in short, poverty. Social hostility – with its roots in religious condemnation – to sex and childbirth outside marriage leaves a stigma, and the result is economic punishment: moral conservatives are reluctant to 'subsidize the irresponsibility' of unmarried women and teenage girls who get pregnant, even more so when they do it more than once. This reluctance amounts, one is obliged to say, to a Canute-like opposition to biological forces. It is in animal nature to mate, and hence sometimes to reproduce; only human animals try to control sexual activity and reproduction for social, religious or moral reasons; and only humans punish deviation from what they have decided, in some place at some point in history, to regard as a norm.

As this point iterates, conservatives use their ideal of the family to promote and justify their views about sex, drugs, abortion and society at large. On each of these questions the 'family values' view is as disputable as its view of the family itself. I consider them in turn.

Sex and Morals

If sexual activity were allowed its natural place in human life it would consume less time and energy than it now does. Sex occupies an absurdly inflated part of the moral horizon, and in many respects is surrounded by muddle and even misery, because prohibitions, anxieties and what amounts to social rationing exaggerate its importance ('the hungry individual thinks only of food'), and in some cases distort it – for frustrated instincts are more prone to seek unusual, sometimes harmful, outlets than more easily satisfiable ones.

The kindness of nature has made sexual activity pleasurable, not just to encourage reproduction but to promote bonding and, plausibly, health also. Our closest primate relatives, bonobo chimpanzees, enjoy frequent sexual encounters as a means of bonding and recreation, just as with humans. Among other primates mating activity is governed by the oestrus cycle, which renders female sexual interest periodic. Otherwise chimpanzees, gorillas, and ourang-outangs do not moralize, still less agonize, about sex, but simply get on with it when hormones prompt.

Matters are greatly more complex with humans, of course, and there is no clear answer to the question: what is the 'natural place' of sex in human life? A woman's potential investment in sexual activity, with its possible sequels of pregnancy and childcare, is so heavy that it seems natural to expect her to be more circumspect than a man about engaging in sex – at very least, when contraception is unavailable or unreliable. If some characteristic kinds of male homosexual activity are any guide to male sexuality in general, men are rather like bonobos in being apt to engage in frequent casual sexual encounters, with little emotional commitment. On this view, the argument might be that heterosexual males differ from their homosexual brothers only in having, as a rule, less opportunity for sex, owing to conventions and the restraints imposed by potential partners.

Studies suggest that, if women's potential investment in sex is reduced by effective contraception and greater economic independence, their behaviour changes. In particular, wherever women attain equal status in business and the professions, their sexual behaviour comes increasingly to resemble that of men – even in such respects as employing prostitutes while on business trips (often female prostitutes, it seems), and in having more casual sexual encounters generally. (The similarities do not end there; it also appears that increasingly many women business executives suffer stress-induced hair-loss).

There is mildly surprising evidence from a different quarter: that over 30 per cent of children are fathered by someone other than their mother's husband or resident partner. (This information comes from two recent studies in Britain.) Parallel studies show the same pattern among birds. This obviously makes good genetic sense; it appears that among humans nature remains stronger than convention.

These points suggest that men and women differ in sexual behaviour only when the latter are obliged to consider consequences. The advance of science has made these factors contingent, not essential; anatomy is no longer destiny. So everything one wishes to say about sexual morality applies equally to both sexes.

Sex and Society

Sexual activity is not morally neutral in itself; it is – when consensual – a good, because it can be pleasurable and establishes bonds between people. But in some societies, chiefly Judaeo-Christian ones, it is complicated by the influence of ancient beliefs and practices. People are more interested in sex than informed about it, and, while ignorance remains, its urgencies and ecstasies make it equally tempting and threatening. Sexual pleasure, said Aristotle, subverts rationality, and his remark is the premise for persistent anxiety in certain religions: if sex is irrational it is a threat to order and therefore authority. In consequence sexuality has been constrained by laws and customs in many cultures throughout history, with Christianity among the worst offenders. In 1800AD more people were hanged in England for sodomy than for murder; in the Middle East adulterers are still stoned to death; in most countries censorship of art continues on 'obscenity'

25

grounds. As a further consequence, sex is shrouded in hypocrisy, guilt, exploitation, anxiety and perversion, adding fuel to its fires and making it a real rather than merely a perceived problem.

Despite the increased openness which has permitted objective research into human sexuality, there is still no widely accepted theory about it upon which personal decision or public policy-making can rely. Yet there has never existed greater need for such a theory, because sex-related dilemmas currently offer Western society dramatic challenges: AIDS, venereal diseases, abortion, contraception, surrogate motherhood, artificial fertilization, homosexual demands for the right to marry and adopt children, teenage sex and pregnancy, sexual harassment, marital and 'date' rape, child abuse, pornography – the list of concerns is long, and even so omits the fact that 'ordinary' sexual relations are themselves still subject to repressive and muddled thinking.

One attempt to understand the place of sex in social life applies to it the theory of rational choice, where 'rational' means the appropriate fitting, conscious or otherwise, of means to ends. It may seem quixotic to apply such a theory to sex, given assumptions about the latter's irrationality, but although sexual instincts are indeed at least non-rational, the strategies people adopt to satisfy them are otherwise. Consider the analogy of hunger: we do not will hunger, but we take thought about appeasing it.

Such theorists offer analyses in cost-benefit terms. Among the benefits of sex are pleasure and progeny; among the costs, the effort of finding a mate, defeating rivals and tending offspring. A simple example is afforded by 'opportunistic homosexuality' among prisoners who, usually heterosexual, behave homosexually because in the circumstances benefits outweigh cost. So stated, the theory seems simplistic, but studies employing the model are surprisingly powerful in explaining differences in, for example, styles of marriage and prostitution in different societies. One unsurprising conclusion is that the status of women is a principal determinant. In societies where wives are uneducated and much younger than husbands, companionate marriage does not exist, so sex is formal and occasional. Women are sequestered to 'protect their virtue', but men are freely permitted extra-marital sex. In societies where women have high status, as in the contemporary West, companionate marriage is the norm, so that courtesan services are no longer in demand, and prostitution becomes a source of variety or specialist sex supplementing (even, on some views, protecting) marriage.

Such theories provide useful perspectives, but they have not freed sexual attitudes from ancient taboos and restrictions. Public nudity is a crime; public exposure of genitals by a live human male is regarded with peculiar horror; elaborate social and legal barriers control how, when, where and with whom sexual activity is permissible. People are taught to be offended by public displays of sex; a person who might be shocked to see copulation at the roadside will watch it in a film, shielded by the relative unreality of celluloid. These attitudes, as a result not least of religious moral teaching over centuries, are deeply ingrained.

Relationships

Sex both creates relationships and – because of the taboos and anxieties that surround it – destroys them. In Western societies marriage and marriage-like partnerships are based on mutual attraction; what we call romance is, in prosaic dress, sexual infatuation prompted more by biochemistry than by conscious choice. Infatuation is the hot torch that first welds people together; but passion is temporary, and the interesting question is: what conjunction remains when the alloy has cooled? If infatuation matures into friendship, the basis of the settled domestic affections is to hand. But lovers not infrequently find that, when the blaze of desire dies, only ashes remain; and they sensibly move on.

But what of sex and the domestic affections? As noted above in connection with 'family values', the monogamous principle in Judaeo-Christian societies is an attempt to preserve the family, but because of its restrictive view of sex it often achieves the opposite. Monogamy entails 'sexual fidelity', which means restriction of one's sexual expression exclusively to one other person. Historically, women were the main target of this restriction, to ensure that their offspring genetically belonged to their husbands; but it is chiefly in Christianity that it applies also to men. For both men and women it is an unnatural and unkind arrangement, especially after initial sexual infatuation quietens and normal interest in the wider world returns. By linking sexuality with the domestic emotions and the social institution of monogamous marriage – along with expectations of mutual lifelong romance, which infidelity is believed to destroy – the settled domestic relationships become a trade-off: if you desire to form and preserve such a relationship, you must cramp or deny your normal sexual expression.

This is an absurd, often a destructive, and sometimes a tragic confusion of two quite different matters. In practice this Judaeo-Christian attempt to restrict sex is largely unsuccessful: most parties to marriage-like relationships have affairs, commit adultery, visit prostitutes, or somehow circumvent the restriction, having to be deceitful and hypocritical in the process – thereby risking damage to their domestic relationships, which is what few of them desire. So in a 'family values' dispensation the choices for combining nature's kindly gift of sex with the great pleasures and benefits of domestic relationships are: (a) marriage breakdown, or (b) deceit and hypocrisy, or (c) an unnatural self-denial.

The principal solutions are so-called 'open marriage', or a second partner (a lover). It is claimed that the former does not work; we certainly hear of the failures, but the successes only become apparent when we read biographies. In the monogamous Western tradition, where sexual attitudes are so ingrained that few can think differently, such arrangements are little tolerated. Accordingly, one has to suppose that the best alternative to hypocrisy is discretion and good manners – of the kind that civilized couples have anyway always practised.

But obviously it would be best if, first, it were recognized that domestic relations do not essentially depend on (keeping up the pretence of) sexual fidelity, and secondly, if society was rescued from the view that one person is entitled to exclusive ownership of another's sexual expression. The painful choice – the tragic conflict – that this view forces is an evil. The desideratum is to live in a dispensation of things where the settled domestic affections are not inconsistent with normal human sexuality.

None of this denies the importance of fidelity in domestic relationships, in the sense of commitment to a partnership of shared life and goals, and of deep mutual private loyalties. Much of the value in domestic affection rests on the security thus provided. But fidelity in this sense is not the same thing as exclusive ownership of another's sexual expression. This essential point is, at great cost, almost universally overlooked.

In most other cultures in the world the problem is solved – except in very few cases, for men only – by polygamy, concubinage or the social acceptability of extra-marital sex. If saner attitudes were to prevail in the West, it would have to be equitably between the sexes; the removal of anatomy from destiny, as remarked above, makes this possible. And as implied by the opening remarks, taking the pressure off sex would undoubtedly make it loom less large in general. Moral conservatives of course think the opposite; they think they would be stepping over writhing couples in every street, which is why they keep the motors of our present unsatisfactory dispensation running.

Homosexuality and Prostitution

Two of the largest margins of sexual life, homosexuality and prostitution, have always been targets for moral conservatives, who for millennia have succeeded in turning the weight not just of custom but of law against both. In the Judaeo-Christian tradition prostitutes were sometimes stoned to death. No single method for killing homosexuals regularly established itself, although hanging later became usual. It is a profound anomaly that classical Greece, a civilization admired by the West and claimed as its cultural ancestor, permitted – indeed encouraged – not merely homosexuality but pederasty. There are contemporary non-Western cultures where similar views remain; in one Papuan society, for example, it is the practice for men to 'supply seed' to boys entrusted to their tutelage, so that they can father children in their turn. This is a literal version of what the Greeks saw in more educational terms (although the relationship between men and boys in Greece was usually physical).

These are customs many will think well superseded. It is a pity history is so selective, though; for just one example of something infinitely more vile which, nevertheless, contemporary moral conservatives tolerate with equanimity – some indeed regularly practise it – consider the genital mutilation of millions of boys and girls which flourishes today in religious practices of circumcision.

The case against homosexuality is that it is 'unnatural'. The argument is simple: male and female sex organs are mutually adapted anatomically for the purpose of reproduction. Since the organs of two men or two women are not thus adapted, and cannot result in reproduction, congress of any kind between them is 'unnatural'. The same reasoning prohibits heterosexual practices which do not have reproduction as a possible outcome.

If this argument were generalized, it would be disgusting – and by parity of reasoning ought therefore to be illegal – to ride a bicycle or blow a whistle, since these activities are not what legs or lips are biologically 'for'.

But the best analogy is eating. We eat to nourish our bodies; but also to enjoy tastes and textures, to relax, to meet friends, to converse. One needs just so many calories and vitamins each day, but one also enjoys sampling Indian and Chinese and Italian cuisines. One may discover a taste for Chinese, and a distaste for Indian, food. So it is with sex. It is natural to enjoy sexual pleasure, as it is to enjoy food; and the purpose of sex, as with eating, is not exclusively the minimum which either is 'for'.

These points show that appeals to 'nature' provide no ground for hostility to homosexuality. The real source of hostility is religious and social, and, as we have seen, only *some* religions and societies are hostile. In them the result is, or has frequently been, persecution of individuals on the mere ground of their difference from the majority in regard to taste or choice.

Hostility to homosexuality has a number of sources, but one of them is that it threatens the model of interpersonal relations at the core of the 'family values' ethos. Hostility to prostitution (chiefly in the realms of Anglophone Protestant Christianity) has the same roots. Yet the irony is that prostitution at least in part flourishes precisely because of 'family values' – as suggested above, by providing one way of releasing the pressures caused by nuclear-family life under a restrictive sexual morality.

In some American states, and in Britain, prostitution remains legally circumscribed, the legal sanctions expressing the opposition and disgust of moral conservatives. As a result it is riper for the hands of organized crime. Except for its financial aspects, the casual, uncommitted nature of interaction between prostitutes and their clients mirrors the cottaging experience of homosexual men, which, as noted, perhaps says something about the nature of male sexuality in general. This appears to be recognized by society, which implicitly accepts what is sometimes described as the 'hygienic' function of prostitution; but it does so in secret and shame, which means that the question is not sensibly addressed, but fudged. It is obvious on the least reflection that prostitution should be legal, not only to enhance the health and safety of both practitioners and clients, but also to end waste of police time and burdening of the legal system. All the reasons moral conservatives have for wishing to control prostitution legally – the supposed threat to family life, the supposed threat to minors, and the fact that girls might be forced into sex work by economic conditions or exploitative pimps – will remain whether or not prostitution is legal, with the one difference that the third of these will always be much worse if it is illegal.

It must be supposed that some of those who work in the sex industry do so by choice. They provide a service which will always be in demand, and, because they might wish to work together with colleagues in safe and comfortable surroundings, it seems only sensible to allow brothels. In societies where prostitution is legal there has been no social collapse of the kind moral conservatives fear. States with restrictive laws might take that fact alone as a reason to reconsider.

Pornography

The same considerations apply to pornography, defined as 'sexually explicit material designed to cause sexual arousal'. In countries with liberal laws on pornography there has been no social implosion, so one main argument against it collapses. There are other and better arguments against it: that it conveys abusive images of women, and involves exploitation of the people who produce it. These points are important, for abuse and exploitation are evils. But they are evils because they are abuse and exploitation, not because they involve sex. If there were sexually explicit material made by happy people who grew rich providing a service to contented clients, it would on this reasoning be unexceptionable. If pornography were legal, the likelihood of its being produced in an exploitative way diminishes.

Some feminists, in unaccustomed alliance with conservatives and the Churches, oppose liberalization of pornography on the ground not just that it involves a denigrating portrayal of women, but that this promotes rape and violence against them. Here again what is objectionable is the denigration and the violence, rather than the sexual content of either. One can make a case against any group being portrayed in any such way; and one can and should resolutely combat incitements to harm. At the same time, it has to be possible that there should be sexually explicit material which does not incite to hatred or violence. The facts again speak for themselves; in countries where restrictions on pornography have been lifted – for example Denmark – violent sexual crime has diminished.

There is a struggle within feminism itself over the nature and legitimacy of attitudes to pornography, and by association to female heterosexuality in general. A premise of one strand in radical feminism has been that heterosexuality is a vehicle of male exploitation and is therefore intrinsically wrong, like a modern version of original sin. To be properly free, this argument goes, women must free themselves from heterosexuality. In urging their sisters to deny access to their bodies – allegedly regarded by men as mere receptacles for their secretions and desires – feminists taught their sisters to think of their own bodies as dustbins and betrayers: dustbins, because of what men variously wish to deposit in them; and betrayers, because women's bodies desire those deposits.

But increasingly there are women who want what feminists want for womankind – justice, equality, respect – who also wish to enjoy their heterosexuality without guilt. One way to do so is to accept the nature, and assert the value, of female heterosexuality as part of repudiating ill-based, harmful, outdated attitudes to human sexuality in general. One source of the oppressive nature of relations between the sexes is the traditional morality of a social

arrangement that feminist thinkers have correctly identified as 'patriarchal' – that is, as serving the interests of a
male-oriented perspective on relations between the sexes,
justified and defended by conservative morality.

Consent and Reform

Everything so far amounts to saying that sex is an amenity
of life which we handle badly and should allow to go free,
whereupon we will soon find it less of a preoccupation.
But the subject cannot be left without registering the point,
obvious but important, that sex is only a good when it is
consensual.

The worst examples of non-consensual sex are rape and
what might be called constructive rape, which occurs when
the consent given is not properly informed or free. Into
this second category fall many cases of child abuse, because
it cannot be plausible to think that children – depending
on age or level of understanding – are in as good a position
as normally placed older people to reflect on the choices
involved. This degree of paternalism is justified by the fact
that, even if some children are in fact so placed, it is better
to start with the reverse assumption as a way of protecting
interests prospectively.

Rape and sexual abuse are peculiarly horrible because
they violate physical and psychological privacy, and in the
latter case trust also. If the one great sin is harm to others,
these crimes are close to murder.

It is painfully obvious that legal and social attitudes to
consensual sexual activity need reform. Given the way law
has been called in aid by moral conservatives over the
centuries to restrict or prohibit human sexuality or steer it
in the direction of their own tastes and prejudices, reform
is especially needed in all those jurisdictions still influ-

enced by their legacy. These are chiefly the Anglophone Western jurisdictions.

Consider the fact that sodomy between consenting males over the age of twenty-one is legal in Britain, but between men and women is punishable by life imprisonment. (Matters are still worse for offenders in Georgia USA; they can be executed.) This is not the only anomaly in the law relating to sexual matters, but since it is in effect a dead letter it is far from the most serious. The age of consent for homosexuals, their rights to marry one another and to adopt children, are far more pressing questions; and so is the confusion over marital and date rape, pornography, obscenity, and prostitution. In each of these areas reform is required to liberate attitudes as much as practices, and to alleviate the tensions that make them problematic.

One of the barriers to reform is the existence of the tabloid press. Its rabid attitudes and the hypocritical way it titillates readers about what it pretends to condemn – 'Vicar in sex romp with choirboys' – mean that politicians, not a notably courageous race, are reluctant to institute reform, having no wish to prompt such headlines as 'government opens floodgates to vice'. The tabloid press subverts discussion of important public questions, a fact we have had to learn to live with; but on the question of bringing sanity and humanity into the law there can be no temporizing.

The tabloid formula of salaciousness masquerading as moral outrage is not however the main barrier to reform. The main barrier is that queer beast 'public opinion', which the media half follow and half form. 'Public opinion' is in reality the opinion of a decided and emphatic minority, whose claim to the moral high ground, usually staked in the name of religion and organized into effective lobbies – as in the United States – makes it formidable. Moral conservatives succeed in giving enough of the rest of us an uneasy feeling that *perhaps* such-and-such is wrong; and a seed of doubt is sufficient for inaction, because few are courageous in matters they have not much pondered, and it always seems easier to follow what appears to be majority opinion than to be isolated. For this reason, liberal reform has to be not just generous but bold.

Drugs

This is an appropriate point to comment on another topic that exercises moral conservatives, because it affords a good illustration of the way conservatism creates rather than solves problems. The topic is drugs. Actually, neither the use nor the abuse of drugs, legal or otherwise, is a moral problem; it is, rather, a practical one – although in a quite different way one might regard the *abuse* of drugs as an ethical problem.

By 'drugs' I mean opium and its derivatives, cocaine and such substances as LSD, 'Ecstasy', amphetamines, solvents, tranquillizers and anything else people use to alter their states of mind and mood, whether they become addicted to them or not; and so the list includes alcohol, nicotine and caffeine. Drugs fall into three classes depending upon whether they are narcotic, stimulant or hallucinogenic in effect. There are many other substances in what we eat and drink that have such effects, but they are generally much milder.

The distinction drawn between substances now controlled by law and those that are not is the result not of principle but of history, and is otherwise arbitrary. Alcohol and nicotine are arguably more dangerous to health than marijuana, and the latter has been found to have medicinal value – as have the opium derivatives and cocaine for analgesia and anaesthesia. So the reason alcohol and nicotine are legal (for adults) while the latter are not is simply that they have been used more widely and for longer in Western societies, and efforts to ban them have proved unacceptable to the populace. The distinction is therefore not a well-based one, so already the rationality of public policy on drug use and misuse is questionable.

Drugs first came under legal control in Britain in 1868, not to regulate their use but to protect the professional status of pharmacists, who desired the sole right to dispense them. Opium was widely used in the form of laudanum, and heroin was developed from opium towards the end of the century. During the First World War soldiers in the trenches of Flanders and Picardy tempered the horrors they faced by using opiates and – as did Freud in fact and Sherlock Holmes in fiction – cocaine. This prompted a Defence of the Realm Act banning the public sale of these drugs for the first time. Anti-drug legislation thus began as a means of ensuring that young men would be fit to murder one another. For several decades prior to 1914 moral conservatives had been campaigning in Britain and America for prohibition – principally of alcohol, but there also existed a British society for the suppression of cocaine. The war gave them their chance; their time had at last come. In the United States the great folly of Prohibition was enacted almost immediately after the war, and in the same mood laws began to be passed in most Western countries against opiates, cocaine and marijuana.

Since then many substances have joined the list. When these laws were first enacted in the 1920s the incidence of drug use and abuse was relatively small, and in the case of addiction was regarded rather as a medical than a legal problem. One result of the prohibition of drugs has been more rapid growth in their use, by the familiar mechanisms of marketing by criminal organizations, and the attractiveness of the forbidden.

The disaster of Prohibition in America should have taught the world lessons enough on this score. Not only does prohibition lay the foundations of a massive criminal industry, but it turns millions of ordinary people into lawbreakers also, and imposes high costs in money and human life.

In the case of alcohol prohibition these developments were rapid; when Prohibition was lifted, the criminal gangs it created turned to other activities, including drug-running. Here development was slower, but as sure. The business practice of creating and fostering a market for commodities is followed by illegitimate just as by legitimate businesses. Selling all kinds of drugs – alcohol and cigarettes as well as cocaine and marijuana – includes focus on the young, making their use fashionable and desirable. All these substances provide relief from the pressures and complexities of life, and induce states that are intrinsically pleasant. Add a garnish of social disapproval, and their attractions are complete.

The criminalization of drugs thus creates an enormous problem where a far lesser one previously existed. By providing opportunities for organized crime, and turning many users into criminals – principally those who become addicted and who therefore have to work hard at mugging or theft to pay for their habit – it entangles the police, courts and customs authorities in mighty and expensive labours.

All these problems would be abolished at a stroke by

decriminalization. What would follow? Would the entire populace suddenly become addicted to heroin? Of course not. Most people who wish to take drugs already do so; most people who regularly consume currently legal drugs – alcohol, nicotine, caffeine – do so sensibly, and manage to lead normal lives despite their addictions and the health problems that follow. Just as one encourages people not to smoke or drink excessively, so one would encourage people not to take heroin or cocaine; and just as one prosecutes people for driving a motor-car or causing a public nuisance under the influence of alcohol, so one would prosecute those who misbehaved under the influence of cocaine or LSD.

I suggested that drug *ab*use is not a moral problem, but an ethical one. By this I mean that people who depend upon (rather than occasionally employ for recreational purposes) exogenous chemical means of attaining well-being or fulfilment, or to escape from difficulties, are in a sad case, either because they genuinely need the support of the community in some respect, or because they lack the intelligence or courage to attain life's satisfactions under their own steam. Dependence on readily ingestible sources of life's amenities, at least in any regular way, therefore strikes me as either pitiable or contemptible. But neither is a reason for making it illegal.

Forbidding people to eat or drink what they wish, or to seek certain pleasures, is a gross form of interference. One must suggest limits, exactly as one does with alcohol: on the age at which people might be supposed capable of informed choices, and on the acceptable degree of the public consequence of making those choices, under the ever-present condition that what anyone does must not interfere with or harm others. But, although there can be justification for regulating matters in these minimal ways, there can be none for forbidding them.

This discussion illustrates two points. The first is that prohibition is a creator of problems, not their solution. This insight applies almost universally. To lift prohibitions is not to deregulate entirely; any group of people who discussed their joint and several interests reasonably among themselves would conclude that certain minimum rules are required. But the presumption has to be on the side of permission, not prohibition; every limitation has to be exceedingly well justified.

The second point expands the ethical remark already made. It is that we may not wish, and in the clearest picture of ourselves ought not to wish, to be people fundamentally dependent on quick outside fixes for our reliefs and satisfactions. This is a point about autonomy: if you are a heroin addict, your well-being is at the mercy of a powder; you are in a heteronymous state, governed by something external. The good life for an individual must include self-government to the maximum degree consistent with its community setting. A life of dependency on drugs, whether alcohol or heroin, is not such a life, and seems a peculiarly feeble and contemptible way to live.

Chapter 3
Death, Life and Dogma

The problems so far discussed are problems about life and living. Problems about death and dying seem even more vexed, not least because they are more influenced by religious attitudes. The lack of clarity in discussion of the ethics of death reflects the subjects's emotional significance; it is no surprise that the liberal-conservative disagreement here is especially sharp.

Euthanasia and Assisted Suicide

Although there are some accidents and diseases that kill people quickly, and although the mechanisms of senescence can bring gentle endings to life, it is also and often the case that dying is protracted, difficult and painful, sometimes involving unendurable physical and psychological distress. In such cases it is not only the victim who suffers, but the loving witnesses.

Contrast the case in which a person has elected to die before some paralysing disease has made speech or swallowing impossible, or before age has leached away the mind so that the remaindered husk trembles and drools, perhaps fractionally aware of its indignities. In this case the subject is able to say farewell, to share the parting, and to go with the painless ease that medical science can so simply provide. It is a devoutly wishable consummation.

Here is an actual such case. A woman in her seventies, agonisingly crippled but alert despite reliance on drugs, considered her predicament, balanced it with the pleasures that life still afforded – and chose to die before these last were gone too. After discussion, her family and closest friends accepted her decision. In the week before the chosen day they came to see her, and wrote affectionate letters; on the day itself there was a gathering, with reminiscences and poetry, and farewells. Then she was left with friends who had agreed to administer the barbiturates and sit with her. As she slipped into unconsciousness they read aloud and held her hands; within an hour she stopped breathing.

This is a case of assisted suicide, which is the best form of euthanasia in that it has the conscious elective participation of the subject. Involuntary euthanasia occurs when someone is unable to express the desire to die, but is in such a terrible state that a quick means of ending life is administered. There are many cases where both forms of euthanasia are completely justified. In jurisdictions where, nevertheless, euthanasia is illegal (even if widely practised; which is almost everywhere – for human pity is stronger than the law), many people are needlessly condemned to suffering by the chief anti-euthanasia argument: that legalized euthanasia might be abused.

And so indeed it might. Is that a reason for letting unrelievable suffering continue or increase? Or is it a reason for so arranging matters that abuse (everything, legal or otherwise, is open to at least some abuse: humans are endlessly ingenious) is minimized?

Opponents of euthanasia imagine that inconveniently ageing parents will be destroyed like unwanted kittens; that hard-pressed hospitals will routinely increase morphine dosages not just in clearly terminal cases but in long-drawn, doubtful, expensive ones too; that the ill, in a temporary fit of gloom, will make a mistakenly permanent decision; that someone will ask for a last injection just weeks before a medical breakthrough. These anxieties increase the sum of human agony throughout the tender-minded West. In poor countries, where there is not the technology to prolong life, the dilemma arises less often. What makes the euthanasia debate more acute is precisely the fact that we are technically able both to kill and to keep alive with relative facility. It is the endless medical dilemma: should we do or not do what we can do? Does 'can' ever mean 'must', and if so, when?

The rule here should be that, when we are satisfied that euthanasia is the right, merciful, humane course, we should do it. It is not beyond human wit to devise thoughtful controls. There will be difficult cases; there could be mistakes; abuse might occur. But that is par for the course in human affairs. The belief that it is mere quantity of life that matters blinds us to the recognition that we can and must accept defeasibility in the euthanasia case as we do everywhere else. One act of genuine mercy, in which we help a person escape agony or indignity or both, will justify us.

Abortion

At the other end of life matters are complicated by our instinctive tenderness towards babies. 'Pro-lifers' make frank use of emotive appeals in describing abortion as slaughter of the innocent. The truth is that abortion is always difficult and unpleasant, for it does indeed involve the ending of a form of human life. But this fact does not make it invariably wrong. There are many hard things we have to do that are necessary or justified – in the name of compassion too, for a foetus always competes with estab-lished human interests and goals. Cases of deformed foe-tuses or endangered mothers seem most clear. Cases of (for example) pregnant schoolgirls seem more difficult; but here the rule should surely be to protect the actual commitments and projects of a present person, in balance with which the multiplying cells within her at most represent a potentiality. Of course this does not make the potentiality null; we accord rights of a kind even to the not-yet-conceived when we give future generations a claim on us to protect the environment in their interest. So *a fortiori* the conceived have claims too. This means that abortion can never be taken lightly, as when it is used for tidying up irresponsibilities in contraception.

But very few women take abortion lightly, and many are hurt by the experience; yet most of them maintain, on sober reflection, that in the circumstances they made the right choice between continuing their lives as then situated; or undergoing the dramatic alteration that parenthood involves – even when the child is adopted, for the psychological burden of that can be massive.

Opposition to abortion is not exclusively religious, but religion is one of its chief sources. Life is regarded as sacred because God-given, so ending it is a sin. This view does not allow that to create a lifetime of suffering is a far greater sin, as it is – say – to require a woman already overburdened with caring for other children to add to their number. It is not the sanctity of life (whatever that means: for it is not invoked in the conservative view on capital punishment and legitimate war) but the quality of life that really matters; and this last figures centrally among the justifications for abortion.

Religion

Because so much of the moral outlook labelled 'conservative' in preceding sections has its root in religious tradition

– in particular the Judaeo-Christian – a comment on it is appropriate. There are no doubt sincere believers who find solace and inspiration in their faith, and who do good because of it. To them the spectacle of religion's terrible record of bloodshed, cruelty and intolerance – throughout history, and still in this present day – must be painful. But religious beliefs do not rely upon rationality for their acceptance; so it is not surprising that faith visits violence upon its heretics and opponents, for its roots lie in emotion. These roots lie especially in ignorance and fear; religion began as the science and technology of earliest man, who, surrounded by fearsome nature, devised explanations of the universe ('it was made by an agency like us, only invisible and much stronger'), and a means of controlling (by prayer and sacrifice) its phenomena – especially the weather, so vital to life. The moralities that exist to ease human relationships came to be enshrined as divine commands, disobedience to which was seen as a threat to the precarious abeyance of storm and earthquake which, as God's anger, always impended.

Thus the source of much contemporary moral conservatism. But religion is in fact either irrelevant to questions of morality, or it is positively immoral. This claim undoubtedly seems contradictory at first, but a little reflection shows otherwise.

In an individualistic society, where personal wealth is the chief if not the sole measure of achievement, a morality that tells you to give all your possessions to the poor, that says it is easier for a camel to go through a needle's eye than for the rich to enter heaven, that preaches selflessness towards one's neighbour and complete obedience to a deity – such a morality is wholly opposed to the norms and practices not just accepted but extolled in Western society. Most people therefore simply ignore the staring contrast between such views and today's comfortable materialism, and pursue the latter. In this way religious morality is an irrelevance.

But when fundamentalists add preparedness to incarcerate women, mutilate genitals, amputate hands, murder, bomb and terrorize in the name of their faiths, religion becomes positively immoral.

Much religious energy seems to be devoted to controlling our sexual behaviour, either by disallowing it (or thoughts or representations of it) other than in strictly limited circumstances, or by preventing the amelioration of its consequences once it has happened. Thus, the righteous write complaining letters about televised nudity, while tons of armaments are exported from the factory next door to their homes to regions of the world gripped by poverty and civil war. With such examples and contrasts, religion has little to offer moral debate.

Some think that a deity is required to provide grounds for morality: 'such and such is good (or bad) because God says so'. But as Bertrand Russell succinctly argued, 'Theologians have always taught that God's decrees are good, and that this is not a mere tautology: it follows that goodness is logically independent of God's decrees.' It might be added that if the will of God is the ground of morality, one's reason for being moral is merely prudential; it consists in a desire to escape punishment. But this, though sensible enough, is hardly a satisfactory basis for the ethical life – and threats are never logically compelling premises for any argument.

Blasphemy

If it were argued that religions set moral examples unparalleled by secular faiths such as political movements, the claim would be easily refuted; as noted, religions fare no better than most secular outlooks, and much worse than some – humanism, for example, has killed no one for disagreeing with it. One might quote 'by their fruits ye shall know them': one of the chief threats posed by religious militants is their use of the concept of blasphemy, even to the extent of justifying murder.

If I impugn your gods, in your view I blaspheme. So if a missionary alien comes to a Christian country and tells its devout citizens that their belief in virgin birth, miracles and resurrection is childish nonsense, and that they should instead worship (say) the horned toad, he would be branded a blasphemer. The alien, of course, would retort the charge on his accusers' heads. And so it would continue, until either he or they were reduced to cinders at some convenient stake.

Blasphemy comes into existence when someone's utterances give a special kind of offence to others, the offence typically consisting in a perceived insult to something cherished as divine. But it depends on cases; and it always takes two – a giver and a receiver of offence – to make blasphemy possible. It is, in essentials, a product of conflicts between perceptions. The perceptions are subjective, shaped by tradition and often associated with cultural identity.

Because what counts as blasphemous depends so heavily on relativities and (non-rational) subjective commitments of faith, blasphemy is not a fit matter for law. Blasphemy laws, like those relating to obscenity and censorship, they are instruments for controlling ideas; which implies, if anything, that blasphemy is healthy because it is an expression of free speech, and demonstrates the maturing of an intellectual community from one level of belief and practice to another.

Chapter 4
Solutions: Education and Society

The Loss of Civility
The foregoing merely samples the contrast, from a liberal point of view, between attitudes to some familiar moral concerns. Earlier it was claimed that the real question is not one of morality, but of ethics: a question of how we can live flourishingly as whole persons, and in ways that respect the choices of others and their differences from us. To consider this point a different angle of approach is required, one that takes into account the medium in which ethical lives can be lived: the medium of an ethical society.

Consider the following suggestion. Despite appearances, the Western world is not undergoing a new immoral age: rather, it is suffering a different phenomenon, namely, a loss of civility, an arrears of good manners. What is often regarded as moral collapse or decay is no such thing; Western societies at the opening of the twenty-first century are no worse, and by many measures better, in 'moral' respects than a hundred or so years earlier: compare (say) Victorian London's sweatshops, swarms of child prostitutes and violent street muggers. Rather, what has happened is a threatened collapse of what makes the social machine function – a breakdown of the mutual tolerance and respect that allows room and opportunity in a complex plural society for individuals to choose their own way.

This is an important point. Civility is a matter of mores, enshrining ways for us to treat each other with respect and consideration, giving us rituals that facilitate our interactions. Youths spitting on the pavement and swearing on buses offer merely superficial symptoms of the loss of civility; more serious are such things as invasion of privacy by tabloid newspapers, and irruptions into areas of personal life irrelevant to public concerns – for example, exposés of the sex lives of political figures. If anything, although our age is a moralistic one, it is not an age comfortable with itself, for it suffers problems in both the cohesion and the latitude that makes society work. The consequence is division, and abrasion between the resulting fragments.

Of course, civility, in its most obvious manifestation of politeness, can be a mask; it has always been open to abuse, and if we relearned our manners it would continue so; but that does not change the good it does. It helps foster a society that behaves well in itself, whose members respect and take seriously the intrinsic value of the individual and the rights of people different from themselves.

Civil Society

The point of civil society is best understood by contrasting it with a situation in which there are deliberately no institutions for governing relations between individuals and groups: namely, anarchy, defined as an absence of structures maintaining a social and legal order, by compulsory means if necessary. One might, in brief and collectively, call such structures the 'state'. On a typical anarchist view, the state is to be replaced by a network of voluntary associations, unconstrained and unregulated by anything beyond good will between individuals.

The central weakness in the anarchist view is that individuals are to some degree self-interested, and not all self-interest is indefensible or irrational. The same applies to groups, such as families or tribes. Sympathies are limited, and so are resources; competition between individuals and groups is therefore inevitable. Competition can, and often does, lead to conflict. So unless there are rules to ensure fair competition and a just resolution of conflicts, the strong will trample the weak and injustice will prevail.

The anarchist's belief that people can live in unregulated mutual harmony is touching but naive. To his inadequate moral psychology he adds pieties about 'freedom' as the aim of the anarchic dispensation; but he fails to see that freedoms worth having require protection because of their vulnerability, and that it is precisely in pursuit of genuine liberties that people congregate into civil society and agree rules. The anarchist's mistake is to think that because tyranny is hateful the state should be abolished. A more rational idea is to abolish not the state but tyranny, by making the state fairer and freer, thus protecting its members from the depredations of the greedy and the vile, who are too numerous among us to make anarchy even a remotely serious option.

This is not to say that the liberal civil polity just envisaged is easy to devise or to run, because the very reasons that make it desirable also threaten its existence. Such a society is by definition pluralist, and pluralism means the coexistence of often irreconcilable and conflicting values. We might believe or hope that such can be resolved by the exercise of reasoned tolerance, thus achieving harmony. But conflict and the damage that results from it is almost certainly unavoidable.

Enlightenment thinkers believed that, by the use of reason, mankind can identify universal goals for itself, and both discover and apply the means of achieving them. They believed that science and rationality can overcome superstition, depotism, inequality and war. This faith was strongly opposed by critics who argued that different peoples have different needs and aims, and that there are no universal standards of reason and therefore no ultimate solutions for the dilemmas faced by humanity. If one accepted this latter opinion, one would have to accept that a liberal society is only one form of human possibility, with no special status *vis-à-vis* others; whereas what our earlier thoughts suggested was that such a society provides the best opportunity for the ethical life.

Here therefore one has to take a stand (as with human rights) and argue that although conflicts and difficulties are endemic to the human condition, it remains worthwhile quietly to push the claims of reasoned tolerance as a means of solving or at least managing them. Even if the critics of Enlightenment values are right – even if the relativist view that certain values are mutually irreconcilable is true, and even if there is no clear answer to how a given present dilemma should be resolved – still we can say that tolerance and reason are our best hopes for maintaining that subtle and constantly renegotiated equilibrium upon which the existence of civil society depends.

Liberal Education

To achieve a civil society, as the appropriate medium of ethical life, requires liberal education. By 'liberal education' I mean one that includes literature, history and appreciation of the arts, and gives them equal weight with scientific and practical subjects. Education in these pursuits opens the possibility for us to live more reflectively and knowledgeably, especially about the range of human experience and sentiment, as it exists now and here, and in the past and elsewhere. That, in turn, makes us better understand the interests, needs and desires of others, so that we can treat them with respect and sympathy, however different the choices they make or the experiences that have shaped their lives. When respect and sympathy is returned, rendering it mutual, the result is that the gaps which can prompt friction, even war, come to be bridged or at least tolerated. The latter is enough.

The vision is utopian; no doubt there were SS officers who read Goethe and listened to Beethoven, and then went to work in the gas chambers; so liberal education does not automatically produce better people. But it does so far more often than the stupidity and selfishness which arises from lack of knowledge and impoverishment of insight.

Liberal education is a vanishing ideal in the contemporary West, most notably in its Anglophone regions. Education is mainly restricted to the young, and it is no longer *liberal* education as such but something less ambitious and too exclusively geared to the specific aims – otherwise of course very important – of employability. This is a loss; for the aim of liberal education is to produce people who *go on* learning after their formal education has ceased; who think, and question, and know how to find answers when they need them. This is especially significant in the case of political and moral dilemmas in society, which will always occur and will always have to be negotiated afresh every time; so members of a community need to be reflective and informed.

Educating at a high level is expensive, and demands major investment by a society. But attaining the goal of high-quality education offers glittering prizes. It promises to produce a greater proportion of people who are more than mere foot-solders in the economic struggle, by helping them both to get and to give more in their social and cultural experience, to have lives more fulfilling and participatory both in work and outside it – especially in the amenities of social intercourse, and in the responsibilities of civic and political engagement. (Recall Aristotle's remark that education is important because it helps us to make noble use of our leisure.) People who are better informed and more reflective are more likely to be considerate than those who are – and who are allowed to remain – ignorant, narrow-minded, selfish and *uncivil* in the profound sense that characterizes so much human experience now.

The Medium of Ethical Life
One thing such a society needs to be is an equitable one, in which the distribution of social benefits reflects the worth of individuals' contributions. In Western society the head of a large corporation earns the same in a year as fifty nurses together do. It is possible that this strange fact is consistent with the idea of a good and just society, where the climate of expectations about relationships between people results in recognition of genuine merit, mutual respect for rights and willing fulfilment of obligations. But it does not give confidence that Western society is such a society, nor even that it is developing into one; rather the contrary.

The aim of ethics is to identify conceptions of lives worth living – whole lives, well lived, satisfying and rounded. This needs the right setting: a society that tolerates diversity, allows opportunities, agrees – in a rational, generous and enlightened manner – where the limits are; and is just. It is hopelessly utopian to expect that, even if an ideal medium came into existence, all those living in it would be transformed. The workings of social institutions cannot replace the ethical endeavours individuals have to make on their own account; indeed, by making choices and controlling activities on behalf of its members a society negates the very basis of ethics: the great tyrannies of recent history demonstrate this point with painful clarity. But in fostering a climate of aspiration towards ethical goals, a society can produce a current in the general drift, which draws along some of those afloat in it. It can educate and encourage; and where what it encourages is the willed insistence on values of reason, tolerance and fulfilment, it offers a beacon to some, and a standard for all.

Chapter 5
Prediction Again

An optimist might say that the liberal case sketched in this essay has a better chance of winning in future because increased literacy and global communications will overcome the narrow and backward-looking sentiments from which conservatism draws its nourishment. A pessimist might say that as the world grows more complex, beset by too much information and too rapid change, people will wish to retreat into certainties, and to seek stability in moral austerity. Only the ancient dogmas of religion provide certainties, and they also provide satisfying and (to believers) compelling reasons for restricting and controlling whole ranges of human behaviour.

I think both will happen; the age-old conflict between the liberal and conservative impulses will continue. The reasons for these historical oscillations are complicated, having much to do with social organization and economics, in which religious moral doctrines have long played a powerful role on the side of infusing discipline into social arrangements. (Belief in an invisible and ubiquitous policeman who sees what you do even when you are alone in the dark, and who will punish you without fail one day, is an immensely useful instrument for governing people; which is why Plato said that ordinary people should be encouraged in religious beliefs because, even though they are false, they induce better behaviour.) But these past oscillations do not make impossible the idea of an enlightened society; there have indeed been, and are, such:

chiefly, sub-societies within society, where more rational dispensations have flourished, sometimes at odds with the law and often vilified – because feared – by the conservative institutions around them.

I know that both the optimist and pessimist are right in their predictions; but I hope that the former is more right, and that reason and tolerance will eventually prevail, so that – in the words of an earlier moralist of the same general temper – we can become, and can flourish as, people who are 'vital, courageous, sensitive and intelligent, all to the highest degree'.

Further Reading

Aristotle, *Nichomachean Ethics*

Berlin, Isaiah, *The Crooked Timber of Humanity*, John Murray, 1990

Dworkin, Ronald, *Life's Dominion*, HarperCollins, 1993

Hart, H. L. A., *Law, Liberty and Morality*, Knopf, 1966

Hume, David, *An Enquiry Concerning the Principles of Morals*

MacIntyre, Alisdair, *After Virtue*, Duckworth, 1984

Mackie, J. L., *Ethics: Inventing Right and Wrong*, Penguin, 1977

Mill, J. S., *On Liberty*

Nietzsche, Friedrich, *Beyond Good and Evil*

Russell, Bertrand, *Marriage and Morals*, Routledge

Williams, Bernard, *Morality*, Cambridge University Press, 1972